TURNING INTO FLOWERS

A Collection of Poetic Thoughts

By Courtney Nahan

DEDICATION

Dedicated to Martha Poore and the late Stephen Poore, my grandparents. To the woman who showed me endless love and patience, to the woman who nursed all of my wounds, to the woman who first inspired me to write. To the man who showed me what a father was, who showed me unwavering strength, who showed me that I could follow my dreams and make anything possible. Thank you.

To my Husband and my two boys, to my mother and stepfather, to my sister and good friends

Thank you for all of your love and support always.

CHAPTERS

INTRODUCTION

I think I finally get it, the reason I've woken up gasping for air. The reason I've found myself sick and timid. The reason I've always held myself back from life. There is always something I have had to say and a million reasons I've found not to say it. I've written every day since I can remember but have kept it all a secret. I've worn my thoughts like chains around my neck, keeping them all in my head where they've swirled with no way out. I don't know if I can walk under the weight any longer. So now, I will swallow the taste of fear like bitter medication on a spoon. From here on I will open the wound and release the words that weigh me down; release the words that make me itch, release the words that inspire me, release the words that might hurt you, release the words that might make you think twice about me - about yourself, release the words that bring me joy, release the words I have a million reasons to share. I hope I can inspire you to be honest; to share your pain, your joy, your truth.

PROLOGUE

Remember me

And the weeds I've had to pick

Remember me and the soil

That I've had to grow from

Remember me

For the flowers that bloomed

Out of my heart

And dressed themselves

On my head like a crown

For I have blossomed

From weeds

To soil

To flowers

CHAPTER ONE
– WEEDS

FRACTURED FOUNDATIONS

There's something about growing up on fractured foundation

Maybe that something means that you grow uneven

One side taller than the other

A part of you that had an opportunity and another
part that was stolen from

I walk through life with a metaphorical limp

I am uneven

I am healed and I am broken

I am ahead and I am behind

I was nurtured and I was hurt

I am whole and I am fractured

My foundation is fractured

THE DARK BLUE SKY

The dark blue sky could have swallowed me whole that night

The way it unleashed its waters onto the hood of my car

It took all of my strength to remain where I was

To not get out and let the storm steal me away

I wanted to be blown into the ocean

Crashing with the white caps

But I continued to drive over the bridge

Staring at the threatened city under the dark blue sky

Wishing I was on the highest building

Closest to the looming clouds

Farthest away from my footing on the ground

I'M JUST HERE TO STAY ALIVE

"Letting go is hard"

What a cliché

More like

I'm trapped in barbed wire

That you wrapped around my wrists

Every time I pull

I bleed

You whisper sweet nothings

And I swear it numbs the pain

Letting go feels more like suicide

I'm here just to stay alive

THEY'VE ALL KISSED MY FINGERTIPS WITH HOPE

I have danced hand in hand with my pain

He himself has breathed down my neck

I have felt the rocks at the bottom

They have cut my fingers without pain

I have fallen into the dark

It has swallowed my soul in its entirety

I have touched the bottle, the blade, the rope

They have all kissed my fingertips with hope

DAD

You've seen him. We've all seen him. The man in dirty work clothes smoking a cigarette outside of an old unmarked building. The kind of building where the white paint is chipping off of the cement walls and the old sign that used to light up is broken and covered in a collection of what flies by and decides to land. The sun is just setting and traffic is dying down. Kids run home before the street lights come on, holding their jackets a little closer against the mid October wind. His old work boot is propped up against the wall, arms crossed, watching the world pass around him, watching everyone return to where they're expected to be. You'd see him and think he has nowhere to be; except for his check in at 7:30 with the front desk. One more time past curfew and he loses his bed. No time for small talk, if he walks too slow the hot water runs out before he can start a shower. And he can't forget to lie down before his roommate comes in from dinner, he'll roll up and offer him something to take off the edge. It'll be hard to say no but his drug screens are on Monday and the weekend is almost up. So instead he'll lie in his single bed against a wall filled with cobwebs and carvings from past dwellers. He'll take out his only possession that stayed with him through the years; a picture with a burnt edge. Two young girls look back at the lens: one about three with curly, unruly hair smiling hard but not as hard as the tall skinny girl about seven beside her with braids falling past her neck. The eldest has her arms around her younger sister in mid laugh. He thinks back to when he had it all, before he knew it was all he'd ever have. He wishes he cherished it more, every smile, every laugh, every time those girls would run and jump into his arms when he got home from work. Those girls are twenty-one and twenty-four now. His youngest is engaged and living on her own. His eldest has two children of her own and a husband she makes promise that he'll never leave like her father did. He promises but she can't help but wonder. They don't think about him much anymore, maybe in fleeting thoughts. Maybe late at night when the mind wanders down dark alleys of the past. He wonders if they could be thinking about him right now, right now while he is missing them so much. He kisses his picture, sits up and asks his roommate to pass him something to take off the edge.

WITH LEGS THAT GO SEPARATE WAYS

It is only dark for a few more minutes

Adrenaline pumps through my veins

My mind is here, my mind is there

My body is present, my soul is flying

The sun is coming up and I'm still split

How do you walk through the day

With legs that go separate ways?

I'D RATHER

I'd rather be shot by a bullet

Than to be cut by your words

I'll die cold on the pavement

Before I lie in a casket of your assurances

LESSONS

All I can remember is calling your name. I don't remember the screaming and fighting though I don't have to remember it to know it was there. The way it echoed up the stairs and snaked through the crack under my door. The door that closed me off but never kept me safe. I called and I called. I was just a little girl, it was all I could do. My voice was so small in a house that held so much. So much tension the air felt like smoke. I remember feeling desperate. Please come. Please come. Finally footsteps. But instead of liberation I became paralyzed with fear. My door swung open and I swore the devil himself stood where you should have been. The monster from my worst nightmares. A shell of a man. Hollow. And yet I still knew you so well, with eyes so familiar, a mouth that could hold a smile and arms that could hold fragile things. You woke me up from those pretty thoughts. You demand, you demand. I plead and I plead. You tell me it's time we learn our lessons. I grabbed the back of your T-shirt and pulled it with all I could. Please stay. Please stay. But you left. You left. And my lesson was learned.

ONLY AFTER YOU TOLD ME

I had this crushing realization

That I never mattered

And I never will

I tried so hard to be enough

To pull you in

But you spit me out

Like I was the worst taste in your mouth

Only after you told me I was the best

NOW WHERE DO I GO?

I could only sing sad songs that day

And write words about heartache

Looking out the window at grey clouds

The weight of the ocean in my lungs

Tasting salt on my lips as my tears hit their corners

I close my eyes and think

How did we get here

And now where do I go?

RUNNING AWAY

Running away as far as I can

Expelling the plague you infected me with

As sweat drips down my forehead

Pieces of you fall out of my being

With each drop my temperature drops

Flashes of times with you batter me

They tell me to run faster

To get away and never turn around

To heal from the sickness

I won't turn around I tell them

Not like I have before

I won't be trapped in your chains

Keeping my feet cemented in the ground

I will be free if I can just keep my pace

Running away as far as I can

WITH A LINE DRAWN THROUGH

I've never been first on your list

Just a small stroke of your pen

A mistake to erase

A comma you forgot

The period you leave off

My name was never there

My heart you never drew

I've never been first on your list

Just a name with a line drawn through

BLACK COFFEE

Black Coffee

And a gray sky

Bitter like you

And dark like me

We don't need creamer

And we don't want the sun

We fit together

Our flaws make us one

MISSING PIECES

I only ever tried to be what you wanted

If you picked out the pieces

I would have built the perfect home

If only I knew then

You were the reason my pieces were missing

LIFE OUTSIDE OF YOU

Choking on the words you shoved down my throat

Suffocating on the lies you made me believe

The only air I can get to

Is the life that exists outside of you

THANK GOD I TAUGHT MYSELF TO BE FREE

I think back to when I stood on that rock

I did something I didn't want to do

I did it because you wanted me to

I think back to when I kneeled in the grass

When I laid on my back, when I opened my
door, when I fell to the floor

I did it all because you said so

Because you told me I'd have nowhere else to go

I believed in you

You said you knew what was best

Your hands told your truth and you know the rest

I think back to your breath on my face

When you said I should have known my place

I did it because I no longer had a choice

I did it all because you took away my voice

I think back to when I stood on that rock, the
first time you ever touched me

I look down at my wrists where your fingerprints will always be

I think back to that prison and thank God

I taught myself to be free

A FRIEND

Sadness has become a friend

We walk together

In and out of doorways

Leading here and leading there

He holds my hand

And listens to my heartbeat

We breathe side by side

And think the same thoughts

We circle around empty streets

Late at night we hardly sleep

Sadness has become a dear friend

Someone I can't live without

EXPECT WAR

Words are so powerful

Treat them as weapons

You say you love someone

Expect a war

A GAME

Time sits still for the third time tonight

It's dark in this bedroom

But it's darker inside of me

I've been waiting for days

For you to give me what I need

I use you like medication

Without it I can't eat

I'm becoming skin and bone

Watching each second complete

Why haven't you thought of me

My mind is clogged with your face

I get sick to my stomach

My body is glued in its place

I'm tying away my hands

So they don't check for your name

I'm withering away

But for you this is just a game

KEEP WHATEVER IS LEFT OF ME ALIVE

I feel so hollow

Like your breath could blow me away

You've taken it from me

Whatever filled my soul inside

If you must keep it

Think of me from time to time

Keep whatever is left of me alive

FEAR

Fear lives inside of me

He built his own house

His residence feels permanent

The foundation is deep

He walks through my veins

He sleeps in my heart

Fear laughs when I shake

He smiles when I hide

Sometimes he likes to remind me

I make the perfect home

For someone like him

SAD SONGS

I take for granted

How much I love sad songs when I'm happy

I forget

How much they hurt when I'm broken

YOU CRAFTED ME

You crafted me

To fit your needs

You made me perfect

From head to toe

We danced in the night

And kissed in the rain

We were perfect

But then you changed your mind

I cracked and fell apart

And when my pieces were missing

You turned and wouldn't fix me

I sat on the shelf

As you crafted someone new

Dreaming of the days

I was made for you

GRIEF

Grief –

Is a lot of holding back the waterfall threatening to break the dam

It's a lot of being in a room and an earthquake suddenly
shaking your core

It's a lot of feeling happy and then a tornado touching
down, ripping through your body

It's a lot of being surrounded by sunshine but having
it only rain on you

It's walking through the gray clouds knowing it never truly ends

REACHING FOR ANYTHING

My head is filled with static

My chest feels numb

My fingertips are cold

My pen is dry

I need to feel something

I'm reaching for anything

A spark for a flame

A light in the dark

I'm reaching for anything

To stop the static

To stab the numbness

To warm my fingertips

To fill my pen with words

I'm reaching for anything

I'LL FINALLY
FEEL WHOLE

Approval, Acceptance, Assurance

My drugs of choice

With them, I'm living on a high

Without them, I'm crashing at the bottom

I've tried rehab

I've gone to all the meetings

But the hold is so strong

I'm not sure I can live without

So I will search for them daily

And when I find my drugs of choice

I'll shove them down my throat

And at my highest moment

I'll finally feel whole

I DON'T TRUST MYSELF

Every time I pass a mirror

I see someone I don't recognize

How is it possible

To never truly know yourself

Where do you go

When you don't trust yourself

OVERWHELMED

You overwhelm my senses

You've become my everything

I taste you on my tongue

And feel you in my bones

I hear you when I think

And smell you in the air

I see you in my dreams

And know you surround me

You cloud me

I drink your every move

TOO PRETTY TO FALL

Like fine art

You hang me on the wall

Pretty to look at

Too fragile to fall

They come and they go

The crowds they flow

They see my paint

But my pain they'll never know

CHAPTER TWO – SOIL

DEAR LITTLE GIRL,

So sweet you are. So innocent, so new. I'm so sorry for the world you came into, the things you have seen that you've had no choice in. You couldn't walk away, you couldn't pack up and leave. The people caring for you were the same people leaving you feeling so unprotected, so vulnerable and raw. Some of those wounds I'll tell you now, they don't heal. Some parts of you are still open, prone to injury. Those cuts remain sensitive to touch, and the ones that close still leave scars. But here is the good news, the other parts of you are strong. Stronger than you could ever know. Made of steel. You persevere, you break cycles, you obtain wisdom few others can have. But little girl, here is the best news of all: no matter how hard it gets, it will always get better. The sun will come up the next day and if for some reason it doesn't you'll learn to dance in the rain. Now wipe those tears, you will be okay.

Sincerely,

You

I'M JUST THE TREE BENDING IN YOUR WIND

I wish I was more like you

Brave and unforgiving

You walk through life

With a bulletproof vest

But I'm not like you at all

I'm soft and easy to discount

I walk through life

Open to every injury

If I was more like you

I'd forget about the hurt

I'd use my energy for progress

But I'm not anything like you

I live inside my pain

My every move is a result of it

You're a hurricane, a force

I'm just the tree

Bending in your wind

USE CAUTION

Use caution when I give you my heart

It shatters like glass

So when you hold it, hold it tight

I survived a fall before

And cracked in just the right places

If you drop me this time

I'm afraid I won't have another chance

SOMETHING THAT LASTS

I wish my hands weren't so clumsy

I've been trying for months now to pick up these pieces

I think I have my grip and then the whole structure
falls apart again

If only my hands were steady and sure

If only they were strong enough to rebuild everything I've broken

Maybe I wouldn't be in so many different places

Maybe I'd be able to create something that lasts

YOU STAY WITH ME

It's strange how you stay with me
Like you left a trace of yourself
Deep inside of my walls
I've run the water over my body
I've undressed and redressed myself
Countless times
But you remain in my bones
A feeling I can't shake
A memory I won't forget
You've become a part of me that'll stay
Until my blood stops flowing with your name

THINK OF ME

When it rains
Think of me
Remember all the things
We used to be

BEHIND CLOSED LIPS

Behind closed lips sits the truth

Waiting to pour from its fiery source

Beneath sparkling eyes hides emotions boiling
under the shaking rim

Hiding in a throat you'll find a voice burning
with impatience to scream

Within a guarded heart lies a love powerful
enough to heal the broken

A little time given and it all could fall to waste

A second more and such a feeling can bury itself deep

Speak now before it speaks on behalf of you

For words can break the strong and repair the damaged

It depends on the strict matter of choice, the
smiles or burns you choose to show

Push to find the rhythm in the lines to be spoken

There may not be a second chance to take

Speak now, scream now, love now

THE THINGS THAT WANT TO STAY

I got what I wanted

Then I threw it away

Why do I mess up

The only things that want to stay?

SUCH A SWEET GIRL

Such a sweet girl

Such sadness inside

So innocent and timid

With big sorry eyes

With pain in her hands

And a tightness in her neck

She smiles and says

She'd just like to forget

AGAIN AND AGAIN

A passerby:

Someone who is temporary

Me

In relation to you

A spot on your bedsheet

A fly on the wall

When my time is up

You'll look right past me

Again and again

UNBREAKABLE

The ultimate sacrifice

Having your heart tied to another

No matter if that heart turns black

Or dies

Tied

Unbreakable

NIGHTMARES

I sold my soul to my nightmares

They can have it

Survive off of its madness

I rebuilt

Grew a new soul from the dirt

DOESN'T MEAN
EVERYTHING IS OKAY

Regardless of what it may look like on the outside

Remember that people have a whole world inside of them

Some people like me have a universe

It can be storming and sunny simultaneously

Planets fall out of line

Tides roll in and roll right back out

I feel things endlessly

Most of the time I'm feeling multiple things at once

And at least one part of me is almost always feeling a storm

Except there's nowhere to run and hide when it's storming

So we zip up and head out despite the rain

Remember that when someone is zipped up and smiling

It doesn't mean that everything is okay

DO ALL BEGINNINGS HAVE AN END?

Here we are

Back at the beginning

The same way it ended

Or is it that nothing ever changed?

Was this fate and I should have known?

Is it that all things come full circle?

Or do all beginnings just have an end?

RIGHT THERE IN THAT DRIVEWAY

I've sat in that passenger seat

And loved the engine under my feet

I've reached over, reached out

Held that hand and left my doubts

I've seen that look, remember that smile

I hold on tight 'cause it ends in just a mile

I've taken this turn and rounded that right

Pulling to a stop in the middle of the night

I've felt the full circle coming together

It's just one moment but I'll feel it forever

I've shut this door and ran to the window

I realize this as I watch your lights go

I've been here before, the movie replays

I fell for it again, right there in that driveway

WHOLE AGAIN

It came today while I was sweeping

The heavy wind of your memory

It blows through my bones reminding me that you're gone

And for that moment in the storm I'm ripped in half

One half of me is where you are

And the other half is stuck holding a broom

Wondering if I'll ever truly be whole again

I HAVEN'T CRIED
IN A WHILE

I haven't cried in a while

It feels like my tears have dried

But I miss you more

Than my eyes could ever cry

SHUTTING THE DOOR

I can't believe we never shut the door

You left it open for me

Open wide enough that I could watch

Watch your life unfolding without me

I can see your smiles

How happy you look

I can see your life moving on

While I'm stuck behind this door

I can't believe I never shut the door

WE'RE ONLY HUMAN

We're only human

We can only be where we are

But our minds are free

They wander and turn

And then you wonder why

When you sit in a room full of people

You feel so alone

THE BOY I'LL ALWAYS KNOW,

I passed him driving down Fort Street the other day. Wednesday maybe. The same street it started on. He was in the same blue mustang we took trips in down to the shore, the same car we slept in, the same car it came to an end in. I could tell by his eyes and his grip on the wheel that not much had changed since. 5 years since. I only glanced, but it was all I needed to know. That's the thing with him, I always know. Maybe it's what people like about him, every time you see him you know. A smile, a warm hug, an endearing story, a good laugh. Leaving with the feeling you've known him forever and that you always will. It's what I couldn't stand about him. Every day was the same, everything was worth settling for. His newspaper clippings from senior year, the big game winning touchdown, his most prized possessions. The boy who dreamt so big left all those aspirations right there, on the pillow we shared.

I've moved on from Friday night lights and homecoming crowns and I only drive Fort Street now when I'm visiting home. I guess I just wanted more from life than everything I already knew. I wanted secrets and adventure, I wanted the unexpected. So I left him. I left what I knew and what I'll always know. I'll always know him. And maybe that's what I like about him. The way he laughs so hard he'll snort or the way he loves so hard he goes blind. The way he drives his blue mustang down Fort Street. I haven't spoken to him since, 5 years since. I've moved on and have lived so much life since. But that boy will always feel like home, he'll always be the boy I know.

WHAT WAS

We went our separate ways

You followed me for some time

Then I watched you take the first turn

I would have never thought

That our roads could have taken us this far apart

When I look in my rearview mirror

I can barely see what was

IF I FALL

I told you

This time if I fall

I know I'll hit the bottom

You felt me shake

When I touched your lips

I made you promise

Not to say things you don't mean

Your smile felt warm

Your words sounded like truth

I believed you

When you said you were falling to

WHEN THE WORDS WON'T FORM

Today I feel like writing

There is so much weight on my heart

Pressing down on my lungs

But today

Despite the fact that I feel like writing

The words just won't form

TO BE AT PEACE

I found your fingerprints on my legs

I looked and found more on my arms

My neck, my chest, my heart

I traced over the spots

And remembered how it felt

To be at peace when you touched me

YOU STILL EXIST

Sometimes it hurts so bad

It hunches you over

Holding your stomach

You wish it would just end

Sometimes it hurts so good

The tears feel like solace

The pain means you've loved

The never ending means you exist

You still exist

You still exist

I SAW HIM IN THE WOODS

I saw him in the woods

Through a thousand broken branches

He carried a light

A light that could challenge the moon

A step towards him

Was a step towards danger

The branches threatening my skin

A step towards him

Was a step towards salvation

His light inviting me to safety

I ask myself

What strength do I have?

Will my feet carry me through the rubble?

If I am cut, will I bleed out before I find him?

A step towards him

Was the thorn on the stem of a rose

A risk I inevitably took

For seven long years

The branches tore at my peace

Pulling me to hell and pulling me back out

I was cut over and over by a thousand broken branches

I almost lost all my blood before I reached him

I saw him in the woods

On the other side of the branches

On the other side of the broken

On the other side of the pain

I made it on my own, my body shaking

But undeniably

His light was brighter up close

It challenged the moon, the sun, the stars, the earth

It showed every one of my seven years of scars

Vulnerable but willing

I fell to his light and let it heal the damage
I could not heal on my own

Slowly at first but then all once

I saw him in the woods

For the last time as we walked to the shore

EVERY TIME

I wish he could feel the fire my body sets

When he flutters through my mind

Like matches and lighter fluid

We explode every time

MY WINDOWS
WERE OPEN

Today the windows were open in my house and it felt like spring

The air smelled clean

Everything felt so crisp

But the moment I took all of this in

My heart broke all over again

I couldn't feel the fresh air in my lungs

I could only feel the pain

Because the day you broke me

My windows were open

DEAR YOU,

Does it ever hurt? I wonder if it ever hurts you like it hurts me. I wonder if it ever feels like everything breaking and crumbling at the same time the way it does for me. Does it ever hurt?

Sincerely,

Me

SOMETHING SO BEAUTIFUL

Standing there

So perfect

With lavender in her hair

Such a pretty smile

With eyes made of gold

Such a lovely laugh

With a ringing hint of pain

She whispers ever so quietly

Touching the flower behind her ear

How can something so beautiful

Be so broken?

CHAPTER THREE – FLOWERS

I SAW MYSELF

They asked me what I loved
I forgot to tell them poetry
Eyes haven't seen my naked skin
Fingers have not combed through my thoughts
It's been so long since my soul has loved another
I stopped writing, each day melting into the other
He asked me if I was a poet
He could tell by the way I spoke
He read my words and my heart lit up
I opened up to him like a flower
The next spring night my pen turned the pages black
The same lined pages that sat stale
Waiting for a story to drink
I am a poet again
Not because he asked me
But because he saw me
And I once again
Saw myself

POWER OF THE MOON

Do not underestimate

The power of the moon

For we are made of water

It pulls us like tides of the sea

Do not underestimate

The power of me

For I am a child of the moon

And you are lost at sea

WITH PIECES OF MY BROKEN HEART

I filled the lines

With pieces of my broken heart

Shattered across the floor

I rearranged them

And I pleasantly found

That they fit so perfectly

The way they circled and turned

To create the words

I needed to read

YOU MAKE ME QUESTION

You make me question

What lives in my soul

Like a moth

You flock to me when I am light

And when its dark

You guide me through the trenches

Am I good for you?

The way I'm bruised and stitched together

Or does my black and blue paint me innocent?

I reach for you as the ocean does the shore

Do I need saving?

Or will my feet touch the sand after I fall?

Look me in the eyes

The window to my soul

Tell me what I'm made of

Do butterflies swirl around my stomach

Are there diamonds in my veins?

Or am I filled with crumbling buildings and stormy skies?

Can you smell the smoke in my lungs?

Or do the stars dance in my eyes?

Fix me if I am broken

Love me if I am new

I am anxious with possibilities

Of what my soul can hold for you

THE FIRST TIME I WORE THEM

I remembered something sweet today

While lacing my shoes

The first time I wore them

I walked along your side

I left them at the foot of your bed

And when it came time to leave

I felt the new leather stretch

As I reached for that kiss goodbye

MR. PERFECT

He smells like Monday. Fresh, like a new start. His shirt is ironed and tucked into his pants. His shoes are old fashioned but shine as just bought shoes would. His hair is cut and waxed perfectly to the right. He walks into work early and smiles at everyone. Coffee, that morning's newspaper and a weathered book in hand. He went to college and graduated top of his class. He's the youngest in his office. His parents are so proud and he never brags. He's a therapist, the kind that is always listening to everyone's problems. He keeps healing stones and succulents around his office so his patients feel warm. He's at every work event, happy hour, birthday party, wedding you name it. He's perfect. Mr. Perfect.

I spent the night with Mr. Perfect and underneath his ironed shirt he showed me his scars. Burn marks in the shape of a triangle. Some on his arms, some on his legs and a dark one on his lower stomach. "I thought they would go away". That's what he told me. He thought they would go away and I knew that's what he really thought. But it's been years and I know that pain always leaves a scar. I touched his burns when he let me and I heard him when he spoke. He used to smoke cigarettes, American spirits. He once went into his father's garage and broke every pool stick he owned. He skateboarded and played guitar. Piano was his favorite. He never liked school. He's been on antidepressants since before he can remember. He even dated a girl for six years who one day decided she just didn't love him anymore. I love him though. Mr. Perfect.

SHE ALMOST STOPPED EXISTING

She steps out

Into the warm summer air

She reached out her arms

To feel the wind

Moving between her fingers

Ever so slightly

She remembers she's alive

And greets the sun with gratitude

For last night with the moon

Calling out her name

She almost stopped existing

YOU'D HATE TO SEE ME FALL

Just a touch of life
You've brought into my body
I breathe you in
Like you're the oxygen I've needed
When I'm drowning in the deep end
About to lose it all
You bring me to the surface
You say you'd hate to see me fall

I WOULDN'T TOUCH A THING

I swear I wouldn't touch a thing

I'd keep the drinks on the table

The minute hand on the five

I'd sit in the same spot

Arrange all the people as they were

I'd dress myself the same

And say everything twice

I'd feel everything deeper

Taking each second and living it out

I'd focus on where your hands went

And truly feel your skin on mine

I'd be sure to remember the look in your eyes

And lean into every breath you took

I'd wrap my fingers in yours

And savor the way that they fit

If I could just go back one time

I'd only make it last

MAYBE

Maybe I'll paint my nails again

So when I look down at the things that write my words

All of the ugly, scary truths

I'll see something nice

Taken care of

Maybe I'll see some love

Or a glimpse of what could come

I'LL CARRY HER FOREVER

You planted a seed

In the soil of my being

And I've felt it growing inside

Your arms are my warmth

Your kiss is my air

Your fingertips are my rain

Your smile is my sunshine

You planted a seed

And I've sprouted a beautiful flower

I'll call her love

And I'll carry her forever

SAFE HAVEN

If you traced the white paneled walls with your fingers, you'd hear my laughter. If you laid your head down in bed, the twin bed that faces the bay window, you'd see all of my dreams. And if you walk down the hallway, filled with paintings of shells and birds, just slow enough, you might find me. I live there, I always have and I always will. I've left pieces of me scattered around the house on Harbour Street. In the garden with the cherry blossom out front, out on the dock that sits peacefully on the bay, there's a piece of me that swings in the breeze on the old hammock we left on the deck. So many pieces I can't ever be whole again.

You see I left myself there so I can always be safe. That Harbour Street house was my safe haven. It's where the wind hitting the windows at night drowned out any sounds of nightmares, the glimmer from the bay blinded the monsters and my grandparents singing in the morning making pancakes chased away my fears. I was safe. Until the day we packed up those brown cardboard boxes, piled to the ceiling with all my best memories. I paced down the hallway, back to my bed, the dock, the hammock and the garden. I dropped a piece of me everywhere I loved and the Harbour Street house promised to keep it safe.

I'LL LEAD YOU THROUGH THE DARK

Stay with me

And I'll lead you through the dark

For I've been here before

This isn't the scary part

WORTHY OF LOVE

The best part is being here

And realizing how far I've come

I've dreamed of living a life with you

Long before I knew you

Long before I knew myself

Long before I grew and closed my wounds

Now living here next to your heart

I know I'm worthy of such love

YOU WEREN'T THE FIRST

You weren't the first to call me beautiful

You weren't the first to tell me it's true

I believed every word you said

But you were the first to make me believe myself

You taught me about peace, strength and confidence

You taught me to live for myself

To let the negativity pass over me like a wave

You've always been honest and pointed out my flaws

You didn't tell me they were beautiful, tucking
them away like everyone else

You told me I was smart and I could work towards a cure

You've treated me with respect

Never doubting my knowledge or experiences

You helped me settle some of the wars inside my head

And when you were the war, you taught me how to end them

EMPATHY

Being an empath: kind of like having a superpower, in a very flawed sort of way. To feel the beauty of the world so deeply but to ripple under the pain of its wrath, to feel for and with your neighbor but to hold the unbearable weight of their grief. It's a gift, sure. To be able to look inward and feel so outward. To touch another's hand and know their story. But a curse, nonetheless. Because to know one other story is to carry the rain, to know the world around you is to carry a storm.

YOU KISSED ME

You kissed me

Right as the joy released from my lips

You tasted it

And told me it was like June

Light and airy

I hope the taste of my joy

Keeps you near me

OPEN UP TO ME LIKE A BOOK

Open up to me like a book

I want to write my poetry on your skin

Be my paper

And I'll spill my ink onto your lines

Sink it deep into your pores

Read my words

And you'll learn what I crave from you

Wrap yourself around my art

Absorb me until your hair stands

Be my muse

Inspire new literature to come from my lips

Bring me to say what I wouldn't

Become one with me

Feel the words written in my veins

Push your way through the sentences

And trace over the letters when you miss me

IN WHICH WE CREATE A FOREVER

Existence is dynamic

Like the wind

You remind me

That moments are fleeting

Temporary

An impact is undying

Like ink on skin

You remind me

Your mark won't be removed

Permanent

Love is temporary moments

In which we create a forever

WHERE HAVE YOU BEEN?

And didn't she stand there

With stars in her hair

And eyes full of sky

I asked her where she's been

She asked me why

NEVER STOP MOVING TOGETHER

Promise me we'll keep exploring

That you'll take my hand

And walk me through lives I've never known

I want to go to space

And walk along the stars

I want to see your home

And wrap myself in the comfort

I want to go to the future

And run my fingers along the possibilities

I want to travel the world

And see love in the eyes of strangers

Promise me that we'll wander

And that we'll never stop moving together

MAKE LOVE TO
MY MIND

I'm asking you to make love to my mind

Touch the only parts of me you can't feel

Remove the layers of fear

Let my vulnerability push you forward

Rub your hands through my hesitations

Open up my emotions

Find satisfaction in my thoughts

Climb to the top of my words

Bring yourself to finish in my smile

Roll over and hold my dreams

Remind me that there is more

Tell me my body is just a vessel

For something bigger than you could hold

WON THE WAR

You told me I was strong

But my soul was not settled

I took my place on the battlefield

I proved my strength

When all was said and done

I laid in bed and found true peace

In the dark

Where I brought the war to me

Fighting my demons

Killing my fears

I settled my soul and won the war

WHEN IT'S ABOUT TO STORM

When it's about to storm

I feel the most seen

The darkness creeping in

The swelling before the release

The light before the boom

Like the breath stuck in my chest

I live in between the extremes

And when the clouds release the rain

I exhale and open my mouth

Tasting the drops and saving them

For the next time I need to breathe

YOU TOLD ME I WAS
THE AESTHETIC

You told me I was the aesthetic

Maybe that's why I came

But it was your room

Your necklace hanging from the closet

The vanilla candles

The roses on the table

The popcorn we didn't eat

The open window

The rain tapping outside

The fan you kept on low

The way you rubbed my back

And kissed my neck as I fell asleep

It was the flashes of the pier

And the way you smiled

That flooded my dreams

It was waking up to your warmth

And everything being where we left it

I'm falling in love

That is the aesthetic

LIVE IN BETWEEN THE CRASHES

Sometimes it feels like dying

It comes in waves

When the tide rolls in, the waves come one after another

Then come the moments of calm between the crashes

Regardless of the severity or speed

I somehow manage to catch my breath between the white caps

A breath means survival

A breath means that I'm not dying

No matter how bad the pain, no matter the panic

I am alive

I realize this time and time again

After the waves pass on and the tide rolls back out

I will be okay

If I can take each wave at a time and live
life in between the crashes

EPILOGUE

Turn it into Flowers

It's raining today

And I think to myself I've cried enough tears

Enough to fill those rain clouds

So that they may rain on the spring ground

Letting the earth absorb my pain

And turn it into flowers

Printed in Great Britain
by Amazon